Stoben

Good Morning, Words!

Scott Foresman - Addison Wesley

Editorial Offices: Glenview, Illinois • Menlo Park, California
Sales Office: Reading, Massachusetts

Part of this dictionary is also published under the title
My Pictionary.

D'Nealian is the registered trademark of Donald Neal Thurber.

Illustration and photograph credits appear on page 143.

Addison Wesley Longman books are available at special discounts
for bulk purchases by corporations, institutions, and other organiza-
tions. For more information, please
contact the Corporate, Government, and Special Sales Department,
Addison Wesley Longman Publishing Company, Reading, MA
01867, 1-800-238-9682.

Library of Congress Cataloging-in-Publication Data

Good morning, words!
        p. cm.
    Reprint. Originally published: Glenview Ill. : Scott Foresman, 1990.
    Summary: Illlustrates words in such categories as
people, places, things, animals, and opposites.

    ISBN 0-673-28510-3

    1. Vocabulary—Juvenile literature. [1. Vocabulary.]

PE1449.G575 1991

428.1—dc20   90-42739

ISBN 0-673-28510-3

97 98 99 00 01 RRW 10 9 8 7 6 5 4 3 2 1

Introduction: For the Parent

ood Morning, Words!
is a picture wordbook for
children who are just learning
to read and write. It is a
colorful, fun-filled way to take
the first rewarding steps into
reading and writing.

The words in *Good Morning, Words!* are
arranged in categories familiar to children. All too
often our language is unfamiliar to children and
even bewildering. Many words, such as *eight* and
ate, are pronounced alike but are spelled
differently. Other words do not sound anything
like the way they are spelled. In fact, our alphabet
has twenty-six letters to represent more than forty
sounds. So it is easy to see why young children
have trouble in deciding what letter a word
begins with and why they often struggle in
finding a word in a long alphabetical list.

The categories in this book group words
according to their meaning and function. The
words grouped under **People, Animals, Places,
and Things** are nouns; those under **What We
Do** are verbs; and those grouped as **Opposites**
and **Helping Words** are adjectives and
prepositions. To find a word, a child need only
ask, "What kind of word is it?" Then he or she
can find the word, along with others like it, under
the proper heading. Each category is also
color-coded and has a distinct visual style for
easy reference.

Every word in *Good Morning, Words!* has a
picture carefully selected to represent that word.
Some pictures even have labels printed in smaller
type to identify additional aspects of the picture,
such as *feather* and *wing* for **eagle.**

The 850 entries in *Good Morning, Words!*
were chosen from a list made up of words,
images, and concepts that children will encounter
in kindergarten. Current trade books (fiction and
nonfiction) and other kindergarten materials (texts
on reading, language arts, handwriting, science,
health, mathematics, and social studies) were
examined in detail to make up the word list. In
addition to these words children encounter at
school are the names of things commonly found
in their homes and neighborhoods.

Published by Scott, Foresman and
Company, a leader for more than fifty years in
producing quality children's dictionaries, *Good
Morning, Words!* was prepared by an experienced
team of editors, designers, and illustrators. A
panel of primary teachers also served as project
advisors throughout the development of this
book.

Research has shown that children who do
well in school are those who are given a head
start in reading at home. Looking through books
and oral reading are important steps in creating a
head start for a child. You can help simply by
taking time to read to your child—pointing out
words and pictures and talking about what you
read.

For hints on reading *Good Morning,
Words!* with your child, please turn to the inside
back cover. We hope you and your child spend
many happy hours reading this book.

Contents

Contents

Letters of the Alphabet

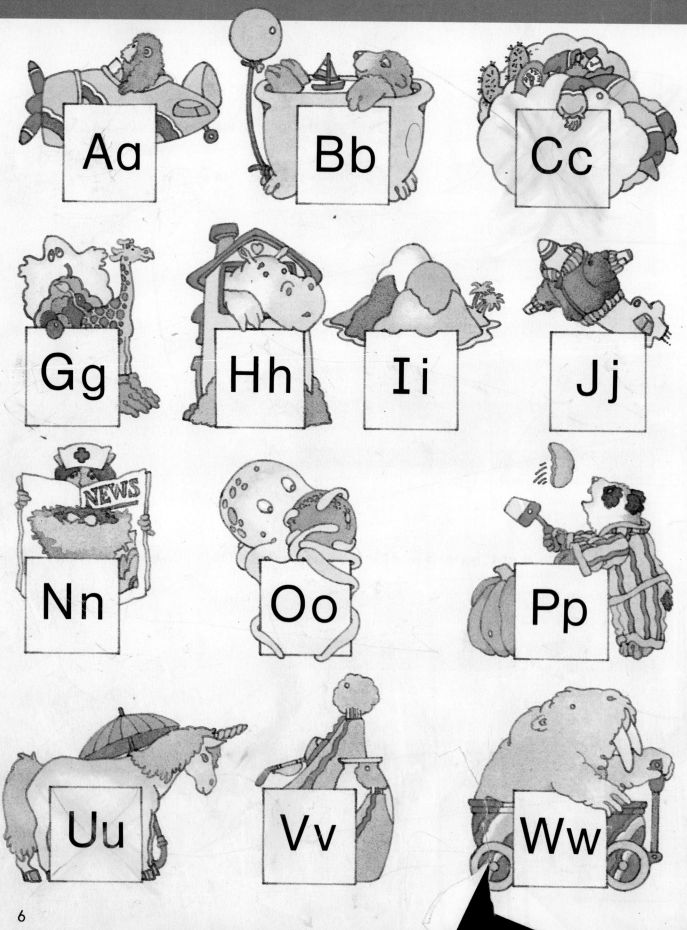

Aa Bb Cc

Gg Hh Ii Jj

Nn Oo Pp

Uu Vv Ww

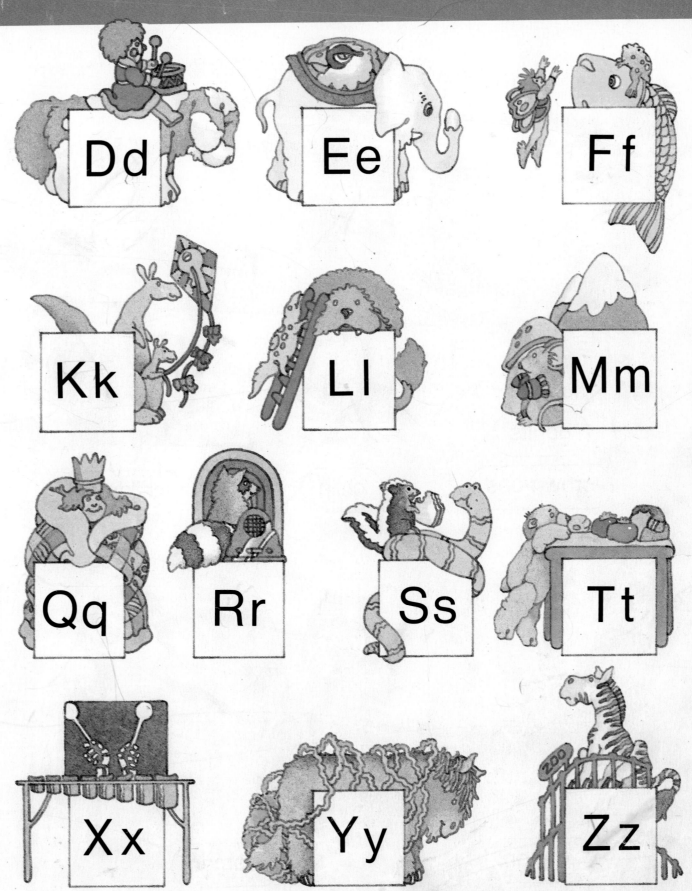

Dd
Ee
Ff
Kk
Ll
Mm
Qq
Rr
Ss
Tt
Xx
Yy
Zz

People

adults

grown-ups

child

children

woman

women

friends

man

men

baby

babies

twins

father
dad
papa

aunt

cousin

uncle

daughter
girl

grandmother

mother

mom

mama

son

boy

grandfather

policewoman

police officers

policeman

salesperson

teacher

doctor

X ray

clown

nurse

astronaut

judge

lawyer

baker

cowboy

painter

carpenter

plumber

electrician

camera

photographer

dentist

librarian

firefighter

mail carrier

soldier

barber

pilot

bus driver

truck driver

secretary

mechanic

chef

farmer

artist

factory worker

face

head

stomach

hip

mouth

cheek

back

arm

shoulder

thigh

elbow

hand

heel

foot

ankle

feet

knee

leg

toe

guinea pig

rabbit

bunny

cat

paw

kitten

hamster

gerbil

21

Animals: Farm Animals

lamb sheep

sheep

chickens

turkey

hen

chick

rooster

cow

calf

horse

pig

hog

pony

colt

goat

donkey

23

groundhog

raccoon

wolf

beaver

skunk

coyote

chipmunk

fur

squirrel

fox

foxes

porcupine

mouse

mice

deer

deer

possum

opossum

bat

polar bear

panda

bear

rat

kangaroo

27

turtle

snake

alligator

lizard

iguana

web

fin

scales

tail

fish

spider

lobster

frog

toad

seal

octopus

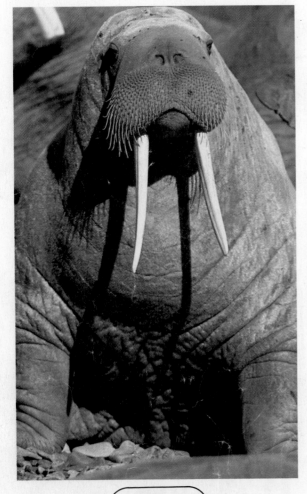

walrus

whale

dolphin

chimpanzee

ape

gorilla

ape

monkey

monkeys

31

lion

tiger

leopard

yak

camel

32

giraffe

zebra

elephant

hippopotamus

rhinoceros

goose   geese

ostrich

bill

crow

blue jay

34

feather

wing

eagle

robin

owl

hummingbird

cardinal

duck

ant

butterfly

caterpillar

fly

beetle

bee

stegosaurus

iguanodon

ankylosaurus

ornitholestes

tyrannosaurus

triceratops

apatosaurus

brachiosaurus

37

Storybook Characters

king

queen

dragon

prince

princess

unicorn

wand

fairy

troll

Storybook Characters

witch

ghost

giant

monster

elf

Places: Home

attic

bathroom

bedroom

kitchen

dining room

house

basement

airport

building

store

hospital

park

zoo

LIONS

library

school

playground

post office

bakery

shop

store

street

traffic light

45

farm

barn

silo

pigpen

tractor

field

hay

meadow

47

Places: The Country

mountain

hill

woods

forest

town

bridge

road

country

continent

world

earth

fruit

peach

banana

lemon

plum

grapes

raisins

raspberries

berries

strawberries

orange

cherries

pear

apple

watermelon

tomatoes

tomato

vegetables

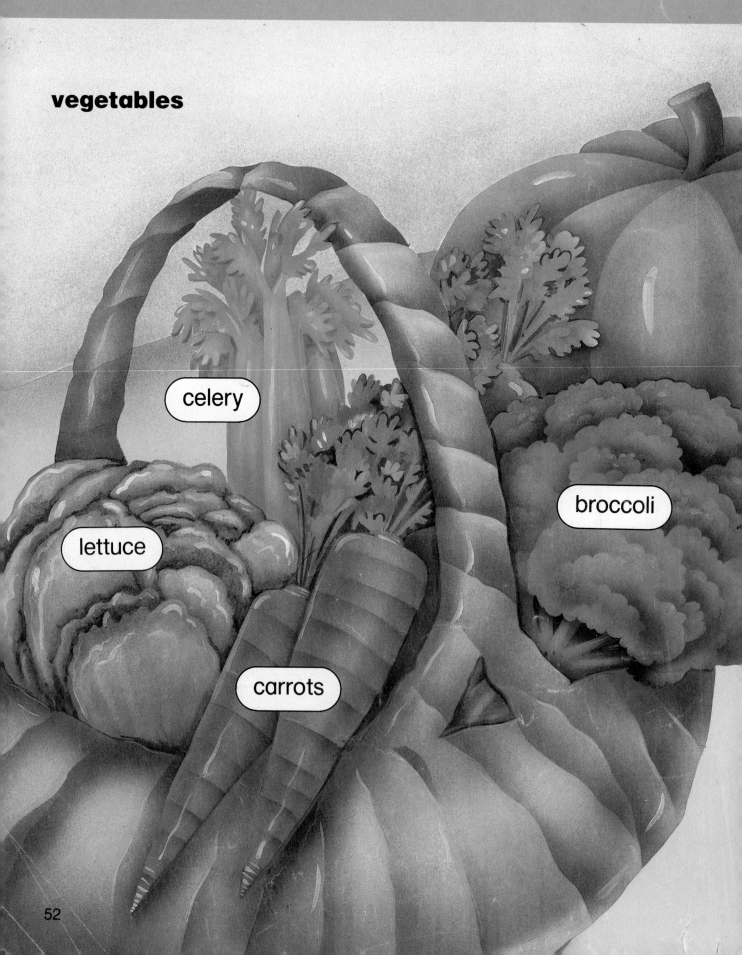

celery

broccoli

lettuce

carrots

potato

pumpkin

potatoes

corn

beets

beans

peas

53

Things: Food

popcorn

nuts

salad

peanuts

cake

chicken

cookies

peanut butter

sandwich

cheese

meat

candy

pie

Things: Food

jelly

milk

eggs

juice

orange juice

apple juice

honey

bread

cereal

pancakes

butter

hamburger

soup

taco

crackers

fish

pizza

ice cream

Things: Things We Ride In

bike

bicycle

car

automobile

tire

bus

taxi

taxicab

train

jeep

elevator

truck

wagon

wheel

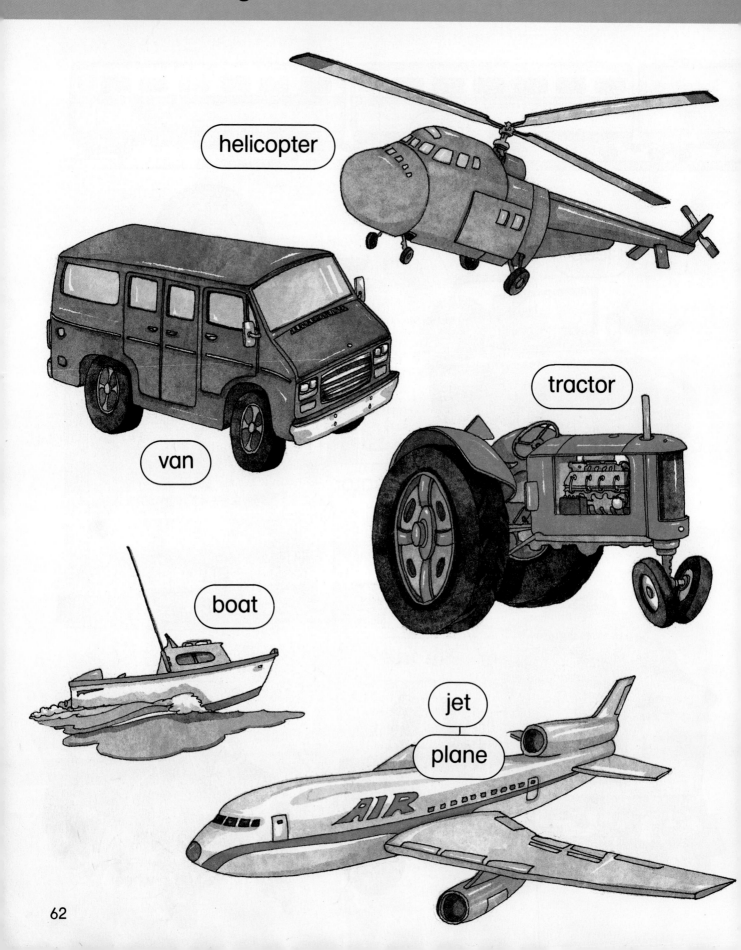

helicopter

van

tractor

boat

jet

plane

ship

airplane

plane

fire engine

fire truck

bottle

pot

jar

dishes

pan

bowl

glass

cup

napkin

plate

fork

knife

spoon

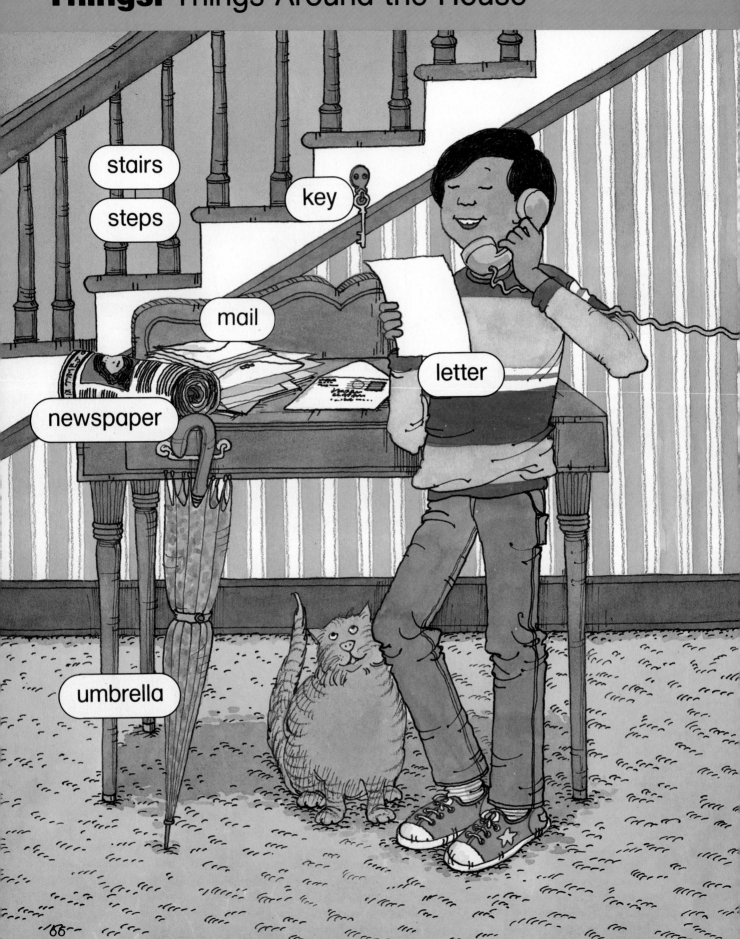

stairs

steps

key

mail

letter

newspaper

umbrella

candle

clock

wood

basket

radio

television

TV

record player

VCR

videotape

tape recorder

tape

record

book

vase

fan

towel

soap

washcloth

bathtub

rug

comb

toothbrush

sink

brush

microwave

stove

ice

can

oven

groceries

refrigerator

table

bag

box

Things: Things Around the House

wall

door

bed

floor

pillow

quilt

blanket

74

curtains

window

crib

straight pin

yarn

safety pin

ladder

hammer

shovel

broom

mop

vacuum cleaner

saw

rake

nail

washing machine

washer

dryer

bulletin board

map

pencil

paste

paper

pen

scissors

crayons

ruler

chalkboard

flag

easel

name

chalk

paint

79

tie

shirt

necklace

dress

slacks

pants

shoes

vest

sweater

button

pocket

jeans

skirt

gloves

cap

mittens

coat

zipper

jacket

scarf

hat

raincoat

boots

watch

pajamas

ring

socks

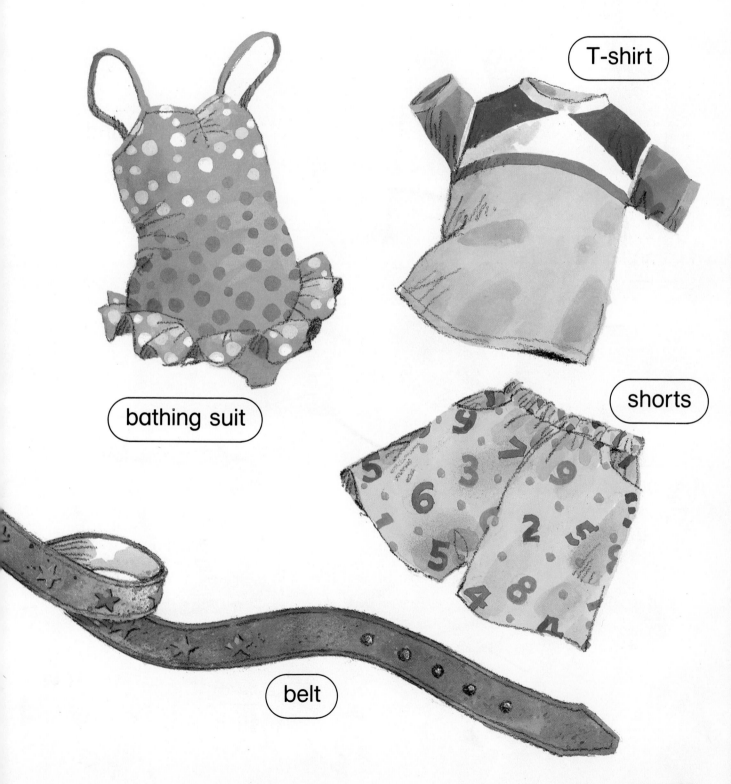

T-shirt

bathing suit

shorts

belt

wind

land

grass

fire

stick

lightning

river

stream

plant

stem

vine

mushroom

root

pond

desert

sun

sand

cactus

90

cloud

sky

rock

stone

shadow

91

snow

icicle

ice

snowflake

moon

stars

lake

Things: Playthings

toys

jump rope

marbles

doll

puzzle

piece

kite

whistle

yoyo

puppet

jacks

top

ball

blocks

game

balloon

robot

sailboat

swings

slide

seesaw

sandbox

dump truck

teddy bear

sled

skates

ice skates

roller skates

tricycle

Things: Musical Instruments

guitar

bells

drum

violin

100

horn

xylophone

piano

hoop

net

baseball

bat

pitcher

catcher

baseball

helmet

goal post

net

goal

soccer ball

basketball

football

soccer

picnic

birthday

party

present

parade

play

circus

What We Do

sew

read

put

build

write

dance

hug

dream

hold

carry

sleep

What We Do

exercise

kick

skate

play

hide

fly

107

What We Do

wash

brush

comb

grow

dig

plant

moving van

move

saw

hammer

paint

TWO GUYS AND ONE TRUCK -- MOVERS --

What We Do

jump

walk

run

fall

throw

climb

hang

What We Do

sing

tie

button

zip

draw

cut

fold

color

watch

sit

trace

paste

Opposites

few

many

go

stop

in

inside

out

outside

open

shut

112

in front of

in back of

ahead

behind

to

from

Opposites

light
day

dark
night

alike
same

different

big
large

little
tiny
small

old

new

long

short

dirty

clean

bad

good

go

come

Opposites

before after

over

under

short tall

old

young

dry

wet

get
take

give

cold

hot

left

right

sad

happy

no

yes

push

pull

123

Opposites

Helping Words

by

beside

next to

between

across

first

next

last

around

top

at

middle

bottom

into

in

127

Colors

blue

red

brown

gray

white

pink

yellow

black

green

orange

purple

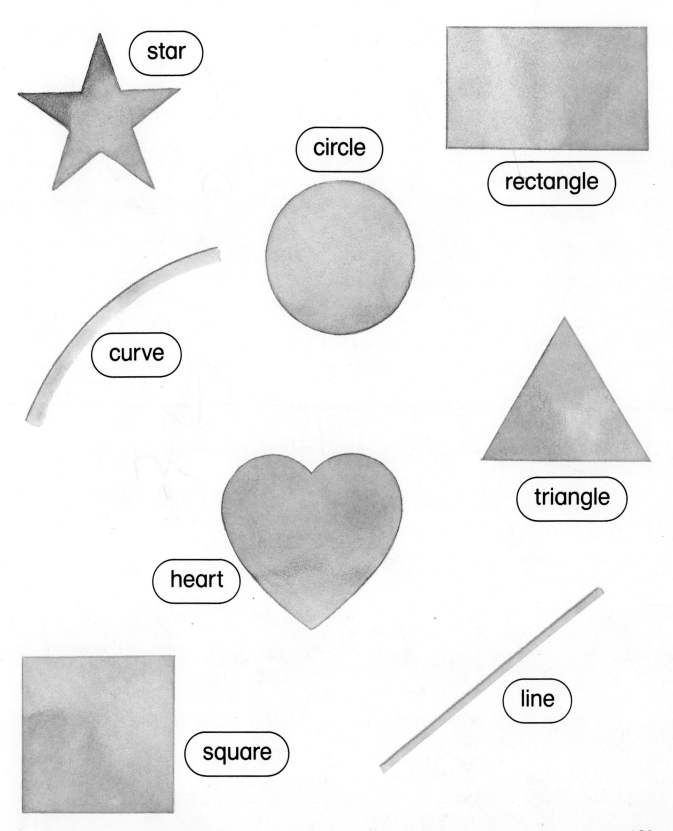

star

circle

rectangle

curve

triangle

heart

square

line

Numbers

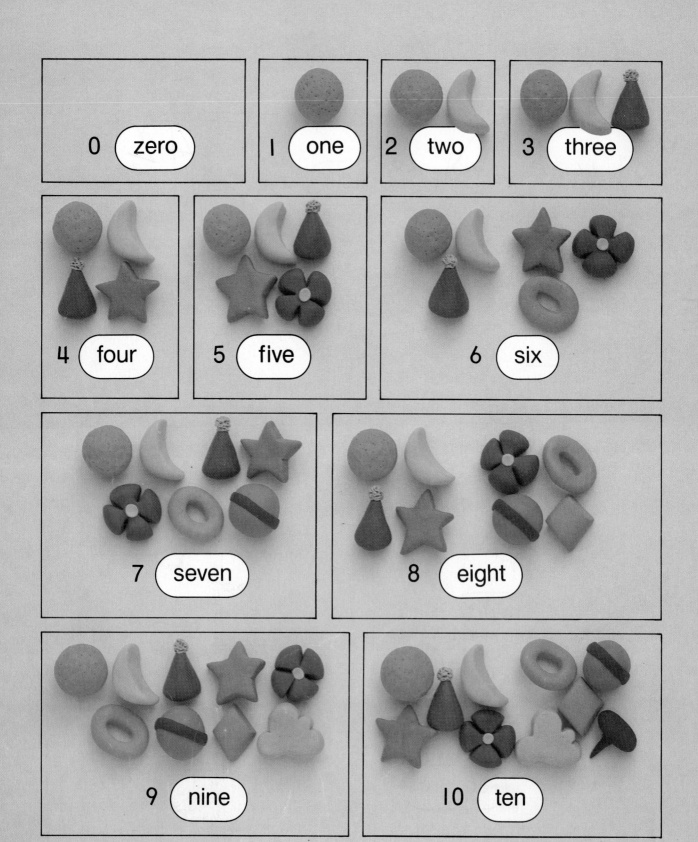

0 (zero)

1 (one)

2 (two)

3 (three)

4 (four)

5 (five)

6 (six)

7 (seven)

8 (eight)

9 (nine)

10 (ten)

Money

penny 1¢

pennies

nickel 5¢

dime 10¢

quarter 25¢

one dollar $1.00

five dollars $5.00

Months of the Year and Holidays

January

February

valentine

Valentine's Day

March

April

May

June

Months of the Year and Holidays

July

August

September

Independence Day

Fourth of July

October

November

December

jack-o'-lantern

Hanukkah

Halloween

Thanksgiving

Christmas

133

Seasons

spring

summer

fall

winter

Days of the Week and Time of Day

Sunday

Monday

Tuesday

Wednesday

Thursday

Friday

Saturday

morning

afternoon

night

Index

Index

Index

Index

Credits

Artists

Pages 6–7—Dick Martin
Pages 8–19—Kees de Kiefte
Page 37—Alan Bernard
Pages 38–39—Chi Chung
Pages 40–49—Linda Kelen
Pages 50–59—Patti Boyd
Pages 60–65—Lane Yerkes
Pages 66–67—Blanche Sims
Pages 68–69—Lane Yerkes
Pages 70–73—Blanche Sims
Pages 74–75—Chi Chung
Pages 76–77—Chi Chung/Robert Masheris
Pages 78–79—Blanche Sims
Pages 80–85—Janet LaSalle
Pages 86–93—Lynn Adams
Pages 94–99—Dick Martin
Pages 100–101—Bob Knight
Pages 102–103—Chi Chung
Pages 104–105—Gioia Fiammenghi
Pages 106–107—Brian Karas
Pages 108–109—Robert Alley
Pages 110–111—Brian Karas
Pages 112–113—Robert Alley
Pages 114–115—Brian Karas
Pages 116–117—Gioia Fiammenghi
Pages 118–119—Roberta Collier
Pages 120–123—Carolyn Bracken
Pages 124–125—Roberta Collier
Pages 126–127—Julie Durrel
Pages 128–129—Robert Masheris
Page 130—Georgia Shola
Pages 132–133—Randall Enos
Pages 134–135—Andrea Eberbach

Photographers

Page 20—dog: Robert Carr/Bruce Coleman Inc.
puppy, goldfish: Zig Leszczynski/Animals Animals
puppies: Ginger Chih/Peter Arnold, Inc.
parakeet: Robert Pearcy/Animals Animals
parrot: Hans Reinhard/Bruce Coleman Inc.
Page 21—guinea pig, hamster: Hans Reinhard/Bruce Coleman Inc.
rabbit/bunny: Jane Burton/Bruce Coleman Inc.
kitten: Robert Pearcy/Animals Animals

gerbil: E. R. Degginger/Bruce Coleman Inc.
Page 22—lamb & sheep: Grant Heilman/Grant Heilman Photography
sheep (plural), chickens: Hans Reinhard/Bruce Coleman Inc.
turkey, rooster: Ben Goldstein/Valenti Photography
hen: Richard Kolar/Animals Animals
chick: Robert Pearcy/Animals Animals
Page 23—cow & calf: Charlton Photos
pig/hog, goat: Hans Reinhard/Bruce Coleman Inc.
pony & colt: J. C. Allen & Son, Inc.
donkey: L. L. T. Rhodes/Animals Animals
Page 24—raccoon: Hans Reinhard/Bruce Coleman Inc.
groundhog, beaver: Wayne Lankinen/Bruce Coleman Inc.
wolf: Stephan J. Krasemann/DRK Photo
skunk: Bob & Clara Calhoun/Bruce Coleman Inc.
coyote: Wayne Lynch/DRK Photo
Page 25—chipmunk, squirrel: Zig Leszczynski/Animals Animals
fox: Breck P. Kent/Animals Animals
foxes: Hans Reinhard/Bruce Coleman Inc.
Page 26—porcupine: Kenneth W. Fink/Bruce Coleman Inc.
mouse: Breck P. Kent/Animals Animals
mice: Jane Burton/Bruce Coleman Inc.
deer: Tom Edwards/Animals Animals
deer (plural): Leonard Lee Rue III/Bruce Coleman Inc.
possum/opossum: Martin L. Stouffer/Animals Animals
Page 27—bat: Jane Burton/Bruce Coleman Inc.
polar bear: Johnny Johnson/Animals Animals
panda: J. L. G. Grande/Bruce Coleman Inc.
bear: Charles Palek/Animals Animals
rat: Hans Reinhard/Bruce Coleman Inc.
kangaroo: Patti Murray/Animals Animals
Page 28—turtle: Leonard Lee Rue III/Bruce Coleman Inc.
snake, lizard: Hans Reinhard/Bruce Coleman Inc.
alligator: C. C. Lockwood/DRK Photo
iguana: Alan Blank/Bruce Coleman Inc.
Page 29—spider: Stephen J. Krasemann/DRK Photo

fish: Zig Leszczynski/Animals Animals
lobster: Scott Johnson/Animals Animals
frog: Hans Reinhard/Bruce Coleman Inc.
toad: John Gerlach/DRK Photo
Page 30—seal: Alan G. Nelson/Animals Animals
octopus: Jane Burton/Bruce Coleman Inc.
walrus: Stephen J. Krasemann/DRK Photo
whale: C. Allan Morgan/Peter Arnold, Inc.
dolphin: Mickey Gibson/Animals Animals
Page 31—chimpanzee/ape: J. & D. Bartlett/Bruce Coleman Inc.
gorilla/ape: Hans Reinhard/Bruce Coleman Inc.
monkey: Rod Williams/Bruce Coleman Inc.
monkeys: Zig Leszczynski/Animals Animals
Page 32—lion: Charles Palek/Animals Animals
tiger: Zig Leszczynski/Animals Animals
leopard: Belinda Wright/DRK Photo
yak: Bruce Coleman/Bruce Coleman Inc.
camel: Mickey Gibson/Animals Animals
Page 33—giraffe: Stefan Meyers/Animals Animals
zebra: N. Myers/Bruce Coleman Inc.
elephant: Zig Leszczynski/Animals Animals
hippopotamus: Simon Trevor/Bruce Coleman Inc.
rhinoceros: Jane Burton/Bruce Coleman Inc.
Page 34—goose: Margot Conte/Animals Animals
geese: Henry R. Fox/Animals Animals
ostrich: Zig Leszczynski/Animals Animals
crow: Hans Reinhard/Bruce Coleman Inc.
blue jay: Breck P. Kent/Animals Animals
Page 35—eagle: Johnny Johnson/DRK Photo
owl, robin: E. R. Degginger/Animals Animals
hummingbird: Alan G. Nelson/Animals Animals
cardinal: Zig Leszczynski/Animals Animals
duck: Donald E. Waite/Bruce Coleman Inc.
Page 36—butterfly: Eric Dragesco/Bruce Coleman Inc.
ant: G. I. Bernard/Animals Animals
caterpillar: Breck P. Kent/Animals Animals
fly: Avril Ramage/O. S. F./Animals Animals
beetle: Hans Reinhard/Bruce Coleman Inc.
bee: Donald Specker/Animals Animals
Page 131—Scott Foresman staff

The D'Nealian® Alphabet

a b c d e f g h i j

k l m n o p q r s

t u v w x y z

A B C D E F G H

I J K L M N O P

Q R S T U V W

X Y Z , ' . ?

1 2 3 4 5

6 7 8 9 10

144

Using *Good Morning, Words!* with Your Child

The suggestions offered here are only a sampling of the many creative and educational activities you can share with your child while reading this book. If your child is very young, simply begin by talking about the pictures. Later, work on letter and word recognition and the more challenging concepts.

Early Activities

 Storytelling and **make-believe** are important aspects of your child's social and educational growth. Use this book to stimulate the imagination.

☐ Look at the teddy bears' picnic on pages 126-127; talk about what is happening in this scene.
☐ Discuss what your child would do if invited to the party. Ask how he or she would feel and act. Role-playing different characters may be enjoyable.
☐ Tell your child a story about an adventure in which he or she is the star. Incorporate lessons about safety, friendship, and so on.

Drawing, coloring, cutting, and **pasting** are activities that help your child develop manual dexterity and small muscle coordination.

☐ Talk about what the children are doing on page 117. Offer your child the materials to do these things also.
☐ Ask your child to draw pictures of favorite playthings (see pages 94-99 for ideas) or interesting places (see pages 40-49).
☐ Have your child cut out pictures of animals from magazines and then paste them under headings you have made on paper:

swim   fly   run

☐ Have your child make a collage using assorted magazines. Cut and paste pictures of such things as delicious food or funny faces.

Shapes and **colors** can be investigated on just about any page in this book.

☐ Help your child finger-trace the shapes on page 129.
☐ Look through the book together to find examples of these shapes.
☐ Write the words **red, yellow, blue,** and **orange** on four separate sheets of paper; ask your child to use a red crayon to draw pictures of red things under the heading **red.** Do the same for all the other colors.

In addition to the **numbers** on page 130, you can explore **mathematics** throughout this book.

☐ On page 112, a little girl counts her catch for the day. Ask your child to count with her.
☐ Discuss how many fish she would have if the fisherman brought two (or four, or six) more. Continue by subtracting fish.

☐ Turn to page 131 to help your child learn to identify **money.** Ask your child to count and combine coins to add up to various amounts.